I0508831

This Book belongs to

www.ingramcontent.com/pod-product-compliance
Lightning Source LLC
Chambersburg PA
CBHW030710220526
45463CB00005B/1990
9781704607627